TAPPED

by Katie Redford

Tapped was first performed at Theatre503, London,
on 5 April 2022

TAPPED

by Katie Redford

Cast

DAWN	**Jennifer Daley**
GAVI	**Max Hastings**
JEN	**Olivia Sweeney**

Creative Team

Director	**Piers Black**
Designer	**Ceci Calf**
Lighting Designer	**Lucía Sánchez Roldán**
Music & Sound Designer	**Conrad Kira**
Casting Director	**Amy Blair**
Movement Director	**Kloé Dean**
Placement Assistant Director	**Tom Brain**

Production Team

Producer	**Bethany Cooper**
Production Manager	**Zara Janmohamed**
Stage Manager	**Laura Whittle**
Assistant Producer	**Hadeel Elshak**
PR	**Kate Morely PR**

CAST

JENNIFER DALEY (DAWN)

Jennifer's theatre credits include: *Big Big Sky* (Hampstead Theatre); *Sing Yer Heart Out for the Lads* (Chichester Festival Theatre); *Every Thing* (Lawrence Batley Theatre); *The Goat, or Who Is Sylvia?* (Theatre Royal Haymarket); *Left My Desk* (New Diorama); *Safe, London Exiles* (Soho Theatre); *This Wide Night* (The Albany); *Educating Rita* (UK tour); *Gutted, Bashment* (Theatre Royal Stratford East).

Television credits include: *Trust* (Sky Atlantic); *Hidden Lives* (C5); *The Interceptor, EastEnders; Dalziel & Pascoe; Doctors* and *Casualty* (BBC).

Film credits include: *The Adventures of Selika; Bashment* (Winner, Best Supporting Actress, British Independent Film Festival); *Robot Overlords;* and *Fit.*

Jennifer plays the role of Amy Franks in *The Archers* for BBC Radio 4.

MAX HASTINGS (GAVI)

Max grew up in Nottingham and is a recent graduate from Rose Bruford College.

Previous television credits include: *Masters of the Air* (Apple TV) and *The Machines that Built America* (Sky History). Theatre credits whilst in training include: The Market Boy in *Market Boy* and Konstantin in *The Seagull.* This is Max's professional theatre debut.

OLIVIA SWEENEY (JEN)

Olivia's theatre credits include: *Macbeth* (National Theatre); *Electrolyte, After Party* (WILDCARD Theatre); *The Secret Garden* (Theatre by the Lake); *Mighty Atoms* (Hull Truck Theatre); *Come Closer, HOAX: My Lonely Heart* (Royal Exchange Theatre, Manchester); *My Brother's Country* (The Lowry); *That Dead Girl* (Arcola Theatre); *Noura* (Theatre503); *In My Bed* (24:7 Theatre Festival); *As You Like It, Black and White* (The NYT REP Company); *Kes* (The Lyric, Hammersmith).

Television credits include: *Ordinary Lies, Doctors* (BBC) and *Coronation Street* (ITV).

CREATIVE TEAM

KATIE REDFORD (WRITER)

Katie is a writer and performer from Nottingham. She is a BAFTA Rocliffe TV Comedy Winner and was also on the BBC Comedy Writersroom. Her short film *Ghosted* starring Alison Steadman, which she co-wrote, produced and performed in, was supported by BFI Network in association with Film Hub Midlands.

She has various television scripts in commissioned development and her debut drama *Yellow Lips* recently aired on BBC Radio 4, which she also plays the lead in, and was nominated for The Imison Award 2022.

Her acting work includes *Alma's Not Normal* (BBC2); *Still Open All Hours* (BBC 1) and *Mount Pleasant* (Sky 1). She also voices characters for various Radio 4 shows including *The Archers*, *Women in Love* and *Teatime*. *Tapped* will be her debut production for stage at Theatre503.

PIERS BLACK (DIRECTOR)

Piers is Artistic Director of Manchester-based company, Ransack Theatre. He trained on the National Theatre Directors' Course, and was Resident Director at the Almeida Theatre. He is recipient of the John Fernald Award, BBC Alfred Bradley Bursary Award, and JMK Assistant Director Bursary. As an assistant/associate director Piers has worked at the National Theatre, Almeida Theatre, Royal Exchange Theatre, Lyric Hammersmith, HOME and HighTide.

As director, theatre credits include: *Catching Comets* (national tour); *Jumpers for Goalposts* (LAMDA); *Crops* (The Yard, Live Drafts), *Love and Money* (ALRA); *Minus Touch* (Royal Exchange Theatre, Manchester); *Moth* (Hope Mill Theatre); *The Dumb Waiter* (Site Specific – Lucy Davis Vaults, NSDF and HOME); *Solve* (Edinburgh Fringe).

As assistant/associate director, theatre credits include: *Light Falls* (Royal Exchange Theatre, Manchester); *Stories* (National Theatre); *The Writer* (Almeida Theatre); *City of Glass* (Lyric Hammersmith and HOME); *So Here We Are* (Royal Exchange Theatre, Manchester and HighTide Festival); *Yen* (Royal Exchange Theatre, Manchester).

He/Him

www.piersblack.com

CECI CALF (DESIGNER)

Ceci graduated from Royal Welsh College of Music & Drama in 2018, and is now based in London working as a theatre designer and associate.

Previous design credits include: *The Mozart Question* (Barn Theatre); *To Have and To Hold* (The Hope Theatre); *Yes So I Said Yes, How To Survive An Apocalypse, Not Quite Jerusalem, The Wind of Heaven* (Finborough Theatre); *Rocky Road* (Jermyn Street Theatre/Stream.Theatre); *One Million Tiny Plays About Britain* (Jermyn Street/Watermill Theatre); *Five Green Bottles, Tithonus* R&D (Sherman Theatre); *Cheer, Mydidae* (The Other Room); *The Cut* (LAMDA/Lion & Unicorn); *Yellow Moon* (LAMDA).

Previous associate design credits include: *Anything Is Possible If You Think About It Hard Enough* (Southwark Playhouse).

LUCÍA SÁNCHEZ ROLDÁN (LIGHTING DESIGNER)

Lucía is a lighting designer and associate based in London and a graduate from RADA's Technical Theatre BA(Hons).

Theatre credits include: *The Forest Awakens, Code and Dagger, A New Beginning* (Kiln Theatre); *The Gift* (RADA's GBS Theatre); *Barbarians* (Silk Street); *Everything Must Go* (Playground); *Invisibles, The First* (VAULT Festival); *The Spirit* (BAC); *Miss Julie, Utopia Room* (The Place); *The Niceties* (Finborough Theatre); *How We Begin* (King's Head Theatre).

As associate lighting designer: *Cabaret* (Playhouse Theatre); *Camp Siegfried* (Old Vic); *Taboo Anniversary Concert* (London Palladium); *The Mirror and the Light* (Gielgud Theatre); *Amélie* (Criterion Theatre); *Les Misérables: The Staged Concert* (Sondheim Theatre); *Moonlight and Magnolias* (Nottingham Playhouse); *The Fishermen* (Trafalgar Studios/Marlowe).

CONRAD KIRA (MUSIC & SOUND DESIGNER)

Conrad is a music producer, DJ and sound designer, and South London native. His musical endeavours span from producing soundtracks, to producing drill.

His soundtrack work includes music for projects such as *Digging* (Film 4); *Samson* (LAHFF Award winner) and *Momentum* (Netflix), to name a few.

Conrad loves dancing, anime and roller skating. He finds music-making easy and writing bios hard. Black Trans Lives Matter.

AMY BLAIR (CASTING DIRECTOR)

Amy has been casting full-time since 2019, having previously worked as an actress.

Casting director credits include: *Meat* (Theatre503/45 North); *In My Lungs the Ocean Swells* (VAULT Festival); *Margin* (Grey Moth Films) and *Centralia* (RJG Productions).

She is currently Casting Associate to Anna Kennedy, working across the commercial, feature film and television sectors and has recently been accepted as a probationary member of the CDG. She is delighted to have worked on *Tapped*.

KLOÉ DEAN (MOVEMENT DIRECTOR)

Kloé is a movement director and choreographer from London, UK, with close to 20 years of experience. Movement has always been her trusted source of communication even before she could speak. For Kloé, this is a gateway to enhancing the transfer of feeling, experiences, stories and messages that are somewhat unspoken. Kloé's work speaks for itself with her most recent credits including work with *The Face* magazine – *Top Boy Season 2* feature, Little Simz' Brit Awards '22 performance, WizKid's sold-out O2 Arena shows, Reading Rep's *Dorian* and Paines Plough Roundabout Season 2021.

Other credits include working with Little Mix, Ghetts, ASDA George, Marks & Spencer's and Plan International.

Kloé has performed worldwide with productions such as *Blaze – The Streetdance Sensation*, training and performing with companies such as Boy Blue Entertainment, as well as choreographing, assisting and dancing with artists such as Cleo Sol, Rita Ora and Kylie Minogue. Kloé has created work for brands such as Nike and Jimmy Choo. Alongside choreographing for platforms such as *Breakin' Convention* at Sadler's Wells and *Ladies of Hip-Hop* at The Alvin Ailey Theater in New York to name only a few.

Artistic Director, founder and choreographer of all-female company, Myself UK Dance, Kloé has led and created training, performance opportunities, work, and produced events for dancers in London and the UK for over 14 years. Kloé is currently a 2021 Workplace Artist at The Place, London, Contemporary Dance school and theatre.

With a fond love of 'each one teach one', Kloé began facilitating movement from the age of 15. Consistently developing her practice and passing it on. She now continues to deliver workshops, training and mentorship all over the UK and internationally. Kloé has been a resident teacher at Pineapple, Studio 68, Base and The Hub as well as teaching guest workshops around the UK and abroad including Spain, Denmark and Turkey.

TOM BRAIN (PLACEMENT ASSISTANT DIRECTOR)

Tom is studying for an MA in Theatre Directing at East 15 Acting School. He has previously spent lots of time doing theatre as an extra-curricular interest with the Theatre Society at University of Surrey, including writing, performing, and directing short pieces and sketches. He also began directing *The Pillowman* by Martin McDonagh with the society, although this was not finished due to Covid. He studied French and Spanish in his undergraduate degree.

PRODUCTION TEAM

BETHANY COOPER (PRODUCER)

Bethany is the founder of Bethany Cooper Productions (BCP) which produces new writing and family theatre. She has previously worked at Wiltshire Creative, DEM Productions, and The Old Globe in San Diego.

She trained at Theatre503 as an assistant producer and her previous credits include: Associate Producer: *Thrones! The Musical Parody*, *Baby Wants Candy* (Edinburgh Fringe Festival). Assistant Producer: *The Fairytale Revolution: Wendy's Awfully Big Adventure* (Theatre503).

This is her first production for BCP and she has recently been supported by the Stage One Bursary Scheme for New Producers.

bethanycooperproductions.com

ZARA JANMOHAMED (PRODUCTION MANAGER)

Zara trained at the Royal Academy of Dramatic Art in Stage and Production Management.

Recent work has included: Production Management: *Lotus Beauty*, *Folk*, *Malindadzimu* (Hampstead Theatre); *Snow White*, *Milk and Gall* (Theatre503); *Pilgrims*, *Urine Town* (Guildhall); *Yellowfin* (Southwark Playhouse); *Final Farewell* (Tara Theatre); *The Process*, *We Anchor In Hope*, *Fuck You Pay Me*, *Box Clever* & *Killy Muck*, *Mrs Dalloway*, *Grotty* (Bunker Theatre); *Hunger*, *Hoard*, *Sitting* (Arcola Theatre); *The Amber Trap* (Theatre503); *RADA Festival*, *Dramatic Dining Cabaret* (RADA). Stage Management: *Dick Whittington and his Cat*, *80th Anniversary Gala* (Oxford Playhouse); *A Passage to India* (tour/Park Theatre); *Raising Martha*, *Kill Me Now* (Park Theatre); *Scapegoat* (St Stevens Church).

Other: *Fabric* (Soho/community tour); Edinburgh Fringe (Mick Perrin Worldwide).

LAURA WHITTLE (STAGE MANAGER)

Having worked with children for eight years, Laura decided to swap the playground for… a slightly bigger one. Fast forward four more years and she's graduated from RADA in Technical Theatre and Stage Management.

Her recent work includes: *Headcase* (Blue Gravy Productions); *Tails of Sailortown*, *Jack, Jill and the Landfill*, *Meet The Real EastEnders* (Moth Physical Theatre); *Snow* (Tiny Light); *Big Red Bath* (Full House Theatre); *Good Connections* (Extraordinary Bodies); *As You Like It*, *Red Velvet*, *Sunlight is the Best Disinfectant*, *Phase One Escape Room*, *A Midsummer Night's Dream* (RADA).

In her spare time, Laura enjoys live music, making sushi and tending to her ever expanding plant collection.

HADEEL ELSHAK (ASSISTANT PRODUCER)

Hadeel Elshak is a British-Sudanese Assistant Producer at Theatre503. Having recently taken part in the National Youth Theatre, she is now working to introduce new communities to theatre by increasing accessibility and amplifying voices from the global majority and Muslim backgrounds.

THANKS

We are incredibly grateful to the following individuals and organisations who have supported us without whom this production would have not been possible: Allan Wilson, ALRA, Bryan Protheroe, Arts Council England National Lottery Project Grant, Cameron Grant Memorial Trust, Cathy Dixon, Michael Bryher, Ramin Sabi, Roustabout Theatre, The Gane Trust, The Unity Theatre Trust, Sue Holderness, Stage One, Phoebe Waller-Bridge.

THEATRE503

Theatre503 is at the forefront of identifying and nurturing new voices at the very start of their careers and launching them into the industry. They stage more early career playwrights than any other theatre in the world – with over 120 writers premiered each year from festivals of short pieces to full length productions, resulting in employment for over 1,000 freelance artists through their year-round programme.

Theatre503 provides a diverse pipeline of talent resulting in modern classics like **The Mountaintop** by Katori Hall and **Rotterdam** by Jon Brittain – both Olivier Award winners – to future classics like Yasmin Joseph's **J'Ouvert**, winner of the 2020 James Tait Black Prize and transferred to the West End/BBC Arts and **Wolfie** by Ross Willis, winner of the 2020 Writers' Guild Award for Best New Play. Writers who began their creative life at Theatre503 are now writing for the likes of The Crown, Succession, Doctor Who, Killing Eve and Normal People and every single major subsidised theatre in the country now boasts a new play by a writer who started at Theatre503.

OUR SUPPORTERS

We are particularly grateful to Philip and Christine Carne and the long-term support of The Carne Trust for our Playwriting Award, the 503 Five and Carne Associate.

Share The Drama Patrons: Angela Hyde-Courtney, Eilene Davidson, Cas & Philip Donald, Erica Whyman, Geraldine Sharpe-Newton, Jack Tilbury/Plann, Jennifer Jacobs, Jill Segal, Joachim Fleury, Jon and NoraLee Sedmak, Ali Taylor, Tim Roseman, Ian Mill, Jenny Sheridan, Liberty Oberlander, Marcus Markou & Dynamis, Marianne Badrichani, Mike Morfey, Nick Hern, Pam Alexander & Roger Booker, Patricia Hamzahee, Richard Bean, Robert O'Dowd, The Bell Family, Sean Winnett and all our 503 Friends and Share The Drama supporters.

The Foyle Foundation, Arts Council England Grants for the Arts, Garrick Charitable Trust, Cockayne Grants for the Arts (503 Productions), Noël Coward Foundation (Rapid Write Response), The Orseis Trust (503Five), Battersea Power Station Foundation (Right to Write), Wimbledon Foundation (Five-O-Fresh), Concord Theatricals (503 Playwriting Award), Wandsworth Borough Council, The Theatres Trust.

TAPPED

Katie Redford

Acknowledgements

In 2020, the idea of *Tapped* on an actual stage in an actual theatre seemed extremely ambitious. So, thank you to Lisa and the team at Theatre503 for not only staging my very first play, but for keeping this particular fire burning when lots of other fires went out. Thank you to those who helped me bring it to life during its various stages: Harry, for the inspiration (and free office space) back when this all began. Shenagh, Amy and Ben at Script Readers for that very first read along with all of your brilliant feedback. Sophie and James for hotel room read-throughs. The ALRA students who helped workshop it with us. Rebecca, Witney and James for helping us with the R&D. Fleur, Shaban, Allison and Kat for the rehearsed reading at SJT. Katie for your insanely beautiful examples of 'Gold' via WhatsApp voice notes. Dr Sophie White for your medical expertise, Lauretta for not only your attention to detail but for your reassurance. Theo for having the patience of a saint and for listening to me talk about nothing else. Mum and Dad for your constant support and regular check-ins. Thank you to every single cast and crew member of *Tapped* and a particular shout out to Piers and Beth; from Dave winning *Bake Off* right through to Jürgen not winning *Bake Off* (still not over it), what a journey it has been. Thank you for throwing everything into this and for being the best team mates I could have asked for.

K.R.

'How are we meant to see the light if there are no cracks?'

(*My very wise Mum*)

4

Characters

GAVI, *early to mid-twenties*
JEN, *early to mid-twenties*
DAWN, *early to mid-forties*

All action takes place in Gavi's garage in Stapleford, Nottingham.

A forward slash (/) indicates an interruption.

Words in [square brackets] are unspoken.

This text went to press before the end of rehearsals and so may differ slightly from the play as performed.

ACT ONE

Summer

1

GAVI*'s garage.*

A variety of chairs are placed in a semicircle, accompanied by a rusty garden table, a kettle, a few mugs, a plate that's constantly piled high with Club biscuits and a flip chart that has 'Week 1 – Go Get It!' written on it.

GAVI *stands in front of the empty chairs, adrenaline pumping through him.*

DAWN *and* JEN *are sitting amongst the chairs, wearing oversized T-shirts that say, 'Go Get It!'*

The three of them wait in silence. DAWN *unwraps a biscuit and eats it. It's all a bit tense.*

DAWN. To be fair, I think *Bake Off* starts tonight.

    Beat.

JEN. Doesn't start until eight though, does it?

GAVI. No.   DAWN. No.

    Maybe we should just start? Can always recap when everyone else gets here.

    DAWN *picks up a bucket and gives it a little swing.*

DAWN. When you said we'd be doing bucket lists, I didn't think you meant literally!

GAVI. They're on standby. You know my bathroom floor? Yeah, it's sort of not really there any more.

DAWN. Bloody hell.

GAVI. Dodgy shower, few leaks... what you gonna do?

JEN....Call a plumber?

GAVI. Nah it's cool –

DAWN. Just ask Stu –

GAVI. I'll sort it.

> GAVI *jumps around a bit, taking short, sharp breaths –*
> *getting himself into the zone.*

Right! Let's do this, shall we?

> *His big moment. He speaks with passion and enthusiasm –*
> *he's clearly rehearsed it.*

Ladies and... welcome to Go Get It! Stapleford's very own
motivational meetings. A haven, a family, a community. Here
to inspire, create and motivate. Let me ask you, how would
you like a life that is rich with possibilities, excitement and
opportunities? Life is precious, so be honest with yourself,
do you spend your days truly embracing it? Or do you spend
your days comparing yourself to others? Aimlessly scrolling
through social media whenever you – ?

> DAWN's *alarm goes off, a harsh and unpleasant horn-like*
> *sound.*

DAWN. Sorry, I thought I'd switched that...

> *She turns it off.*

Sorry Gavi.

GAVI. No worries. So do you, do you...

> *He loses track.*

JEN. Scroll.

GAVI. Do you aimlessly scroll through social media whenever
you get a minute to yourself? We're becoming like robots.
We are going through life forgetting our purposes, our
passions, our *raison d'être.* Yesterday is the past, tomorrow
is the future, today is a gift and that, my friends, is why they
call it the present.

DAWN. I've got that on a fridge magnet.

GAVI. So that's why together – and this is the exciting bit –
we're gonna change that here at Go Get It. Right here.
Right now.

*He fist-pumps the air again, whooping. He turns the flip
chart over to a page that says 'GOALS'.*

So today, we're gonna tackle the big G… Goals! Dawn,
when was the last time you pushed yourself out of your
comfort zone?

JEN. Last week she did her big shop at Morrisons instead of
ASDA.

DAWN. I can live out of my comfort zone.

JEN. When?

DAWN thinks.

DAWN. Went to that Latin dance class on my own.

GAVI. Yes Dawn! And did you enjoy it?

DAWN. Hated it.

GAVI. But you went alone! That says a lot about you.

JEN. Only 'cause Stef dropped out at the last minute. Dad
literally had to shove her out the door.

DAWN. And when was the last time you put yourself out of
your comfort zone?

JEN. Every day since living back with you.

GAVI enthusiastically taps the board.

GAVI. Dawn, here at Go Get It, I'd like you to achieve
something that scares you, that inspires you, that challenges
you. So, by the end of our first term in six weeks' time, what
is the one thing you'd like to achieve?

She goes to speak but hesitates.

This is a safe space.

DAWN *takes a deep breath and stands up.*

JEN. What you standing up / for?

DAWN. I want to start a little… group.

JEN *hangs her head.*

Forget it.

GAVI. No, go on! What sort of group?

DAWN.…A paranormal one.

GAVI. Paranormal…? Right. Great!

Sorry, when you say 'paranormal', what exactly does that involve?

JEN. Absolute nutters.

DAWN. Oh, I'm not talking about it. Not whilst she's here. (*To* JEN.) You're just like your dad.

JEN. What, sane?

DAWN. Small-minded.

JEN. Ever since Mum went to see Psychic Sandra at The Feathers Tavern, she's convinced our house is haunted. Even though it was built in 1981.

DAWN. It's not the age, it's the energy. (*To* GAVI.) See? This is what I have to put up with day in, day out. My dreams being shattered by her and Stu.

JEN *rolls her eyes.*

Every night for the last few weeks, at around 2.30 a.m., I've been woken up by this tugging on the covers… Otis would always tug at the covers when he wanted to go out. And what time did he die? 2.30.

GAVI. Otis as in your –

JEN. Dead cat.

DAWN. Explain that.

GAVI. ... Right, okay, so with this paranormal group, what can we do to help you?

DAWN. Turn up?

GAVI. I meant more in terms of resources.

DAWN. Well, I'd need a venue. And people. I've got all the tools already.

GAVI. Tools?

DAWN. Yeah, to contact them.

GAVI. Them?

JEN. The spirits Gavi, come on, keep up.

GAVI *writes on the flip chart 'Dawn – Goal – Paranormal Group'.*

GAVI. Okay! Dawn, you have six weeks to achieve your goal. And if you don't, you need to pledge a hundred quid.

DAWN (*outraged*). Who to?

GAVI. Charity! By giving you a cost of an action, it'll just subconsciously spur you on.

DAWN. I struggle enough with my big shop, let alone pledging a spare hundred quid.

GAVI. Stick to your goal then.

DAWN. Fine. You're on.

GAVI *fist-pumps* DAWN.

GAVI. Jen! Six weeks. What do you want to achieve?

JEN. To be out of this shit hole.

GAVI. ... Anything a bit more specific?

DAWN. Funny how it was never a 'shit hole' when you lived with him.

JEN *refuses to rise to it.*

You wanna get back to your singing. Gavi, you should hear her –

GAVI. I have.

DAWN. You know what you wanna do, you wanna speak to Jackie Brewer. Look at what happened to her career after Stapleford's Got Talent.

JEN. I'd hardly say singing at The Feathers Tavern every Friday night counts as a career.

DAWN. It's more than what you're doing.

JEN stands up, putting her work fleece on.

JEN. Well, this has all been really enlightening.

DAWN. Where are you going?

JEN. See if Dad wants a beer before his shift.

DAWN. Ta for the invite.

JEN goes to leave.

Jen!

She nods towards GAVI.

JEN (*to* GAVI). Sorry, but you did say if it wasn't my thing then… you don't need me, do you?

GAVI struggles to say yes.

See?

She leaves.

DAWN. Sod everyone else, we don't need them!

GAVI. Yeah no we sort of do.

They look around at the space – clueless.

DAWN (*signals to her T-shirt*). How about I start wearing this out and about? Help spread the word? Not sure Steph'd let us wear them at work, but…

He tries to disguise his disappointment.

Gavi, *that* was nothing to do with this.

GAVI. Hopefully she'll give it another go, eh?

DAWN. Wouldn't hold your breath. She's awful at the minute. Slamming doors. Answering back. Never talks to me.

It's not very nice actually. Starting to feel a bit...

GAVI. Come on, none of that. Positive up here – (*Points to his head.*) positive out there.

DAWN. You just cope, don't you? With everything. You always just... bounce back.

GAVI *turns over a page on the flip chart. He draws a circle and writes in the middle of it 'Spreading the word!'*

GAVI. So do you.

DAWN. Wouldn't say I 'bounce' back. Sort of... plod back, maybe, but.

Beat.

I'm really glad you're back. Spreading all your... 'positive vibes'.

GAVI. What's there not to be positive about? I'm breathing, you're breathing. Future's bright Dawn.

DAWN (*not entirely convinced*). Yeah. Future's bright.

GAVI *bullet-points his ideas throughout the conversation below:*

'Word of mouth'

'Local press'

'Stabbo Facebook page'

'Radio Notts'

'Billboards'

DAWN. Everyone at Co-op's chuffed having you there. I can feel it – y'know, in the aisles. Enjoying it?

GAVI. Yeah! Are you?

DAWN. Oh, it's different with me. Can't imagine *not* being there. But you… I mean, Brighton had a beach and everything. (*Carefully.*) And the job? Will they keep it open for you?

GAVI. Nah. It's cool though.

DAWN.…Is it?

GAVI *continues to brainstorm throughout the below.*

GAVI. My mum just needed me around more, so made sense.

DAWN. How's she getting on?

GAVI. Had a bit of a rough patch, but yeah. Much better now.

DAWN. I bet you being back will have done her the world of / good.

GAVI. Sorry Dawn, but do you mind if we call it a day?

Her face drops.

It's just, my head's like – (*Explosive noise.*) with how to spread the word and that and… I reckon these sessions will be loads more beneficial when there's more of us here. Feeding off each other's energy.

DAWN. Right.

GAVI. Cheers for coming though. Proper appreciate it.

DAWN. Not at all, I've really enjoyed it actually! With all the – (*Points to the flip chart.*) Yeah, looking forward to all that.

She picks up her jacket and her bag.

Don't suppose I could take a biscuit for the road? Well, to cross it.

GAVI *gestures for her to go for it.*

Yellow Club biscuits? When did that happen?

GAVI. Honeycomb.

Disgust from DAWN.

DAWN. I'll stick to mint.

She grabs a handful.

I already feel quite inspired!

GAVI. I am gonna do this, Dawn. I'm gonna change things. Round here.

DAWN. Smashing.

2

The flip chart reads: 'Week 2 – Go Get It! POSITIVE VISUALISATION!'

There are even more chairs.

JEN. Did you buy more chairs?

GAVI. Yep.

JEN. That was optimistic.

DAWN'*s alarm goes off again.*

DAWN. Could have sworn I'd turned it –

She turns it off.

If it's any consolation, my dad wanted to come but it clashes with his boot camp.

JEN. Plus, he got arrested.

DAWN. He didn't get *arrested*.

GAVI. Jim got arrested?

DAWN. He got his wrists slapped, that's all.

JEN. He keeps pretending he's got dementia, so he doesn't have to pay his dinner bill. It's amazing.

DAWN. It's not amazing Jen.

GAVI. Did it work?

JEN (*proudly*). Nando's, Pizza Express and Bella Italia.

DAWN. It's so humiliating. Especially with the posh ones.

GAVI. Does he need money? We could always do a sweep round?

DAWN. He's not poor. He just likes a challenge.

GAVI. Fair enough.

Right. We can always recap when the others turn up... so, let's go, shall we?

He whoops.

Week two!

DAWN. Sorry, just quickly, Hilary next door said she might come as well, but she's had a lot going on. I won't go into it, it's not my place, but...

GAVI. Ah. I hope she's alright. Okay! So, week / two! –

DAWN. Jacob, her son – year below you at school, used to burp all the time, he was off work due to anxiety, so moved back in with her. Kept screaming in the night and that, must have been terrifying, but she was ever so good with him. Anyway, he's doing much better now. He's got a job at Halfords and signed up for a half marathon.

Beat.

JEN. What happened to not going into it?

DAWN. Hilary's not exactly discreet herself.

JEN. She wouldn't be sitting there, spreading your shit around.

DAWN. She would.

JEN. She wouldn't.

DAWN. Well then why did she tell Stef she saw your car outside Mike's last week?

GAVI. So, week two! This week, / we're going to –

JEN. Hilary can mind her pissing business. And Stef. They can / all just –

DAWN. Don't bring Stef into this. You wouldn't have a job if it wasn't for her.

JEN. Yeah, I'm dead grateful to Stef for giving me the opportunity to stack shelves with beans and rice fucking pudding.

DAWN. Sometimes, I struggle to comprehend the fact I made you.

JEN. So do I Mum, so do I.

DAWN. I just – I – I don't understand why you have to be so –

Suddenly, we hear 'Gold' by Spandau Ballet play loudly through GAVI's *bluetooth speakers. He closes his eyes, transfixed.*

DAWN *and* JEN *watch him, unsure of what's happening.*

After a while, he stops the music.

GAVI. Okay, so Jen, before, we move on –

JEN. Sorry, what the fuck was that?

GAVI. Just a little… boost.

They're still baffled. GAVI *turns the page back to 'GOALS' on the flip chart.*

Jen. Before we move on with this week's task, what are you hoping to achieve by the end of our first term?

JEN *(reiterating)*.…To get out of this shit hole.

DAWN. It's not that shit. Lots of exciting things have happened round here.

JEN. Name *one* exciting thing that's happened round here.

Silence.

GAVI. Bradley Walsh opened Domino's.

JEN *rests her case*.

Any thoughts as to where you want to go?

JEN. Madrid.

GAVI (*taken aback*). Madrid?

DAWN. *Madrid?* You can't speak Spanish!

JEN. There's this job at a bar, and –

DAWN. You're moving all the way to Madrid to pull pints?

JEN (*slightly hesitant*). No! It's – this bar – they're looking for like, an English singer – sort of thing, so…

DAWN. Well, have you got it?

JEN. No, I've got to audition –

DAWN. What, in Madrid?

JEN. No, in London.

DAWN. *London?!*

JEN. Yes, London.

DAWN. Well where will you live? How much will you get paid? And you hate paella. You threw it all back up after Stef's Eurovision party.

JEN. I was like seven! Anyway, what's the problem, I thought you wanted me gone?

GAVI. Course she doesn't! It's just mother's prerogative and that.

JEN. That's finally kicked in, has it?

GAVI. When's the audition?

JEN. Next month. Said if I get it, I could pretty much move straight away.

DAWN. Well it's a month's notice you've got to give at the Co-Op, so are you going to consider that?

JEN. Nope.

GAVI *writes on the flip chart – 'Jen – Goal – Madrid!'*

GAVI. Do you want any help with it? Like, rehearsals? Mental preparation? Sort of my thing.

JEN *nods, appreciatively.*

Madrid! Bloody hell.

Okay, so, now we've established both of your goals…

GAVI *flips over the page. There's a list of activities on the list:*

'Buy a stranger a coffee.'

'Get on a bus without knowing where it's going.'

'Have cold showers every morning for a week.'

'Write a poem.'

'Paint a picture.'

'Swim in a pond.'

Here are the tasks to help get you there! Dawn?

DAWN's *consumed by the recent announcement.*

Pick one. Any one.

She tries to digest the tasks.

DAWN. 'Get on a bus without knowing where it's going'… won't be good for my nerves. 'Have cold showers every morning' – I'm not mad…

JEN. We don't need a running commentary, Mum.

DAWN. I do like coffee.

GAVI. It's yours! Well, a stranger's. Jen?

JEN *isn't convinced.*

By doing small tasks like this can help you remove yourself from your comfort zone until eventually, you'll be conquering the world!

JEN. No offence but freezing my tits off by having cold showers isn't gonna get me to Madrid.

GAVI. Cold showers. It's yours! Now, for the exciting stuff… Positive Visualisation!

GAVI turns to the original page on the flip chart that says, 'POSITIVE VISUALISATION!'

DAWN. Don't talk to me about positive visualisation!

GAVI. Well, I'm just about to, so –

DAWN. I swear by it. Made a scrapbook when I was younger, full of things I wished for and let me tell you, the stuff in there is the life I am living right now.

JEN. You wished for *this*?

DAWN (*ignoring her*). I stuck a picture of a seaside in there because I wanted to live by the sea. Moved into a house with a pond. Put a picture of a hospital in there because I wanted to marry a doctor. Didn't marry a doctor, but… what did my initials become when I married Stu?

Beat.

D… R. And this is the best bit.

She pulls out her purse and unfolds a picture from it of a man, a woman and a young girl.

I've carried this on me for years; always wanted my own family – (*Points.*) a mum, a dad and a daughter.

She smiles.

So, it does work.

Beat.

JEN. Sorry, who are they?

DAWN. I don't know, but the point is, I liked it, I visualised it, I got it.

JEN. So, you're just carrying around a photo of a random family instead of your actual one?

DAWN. Came for free with the frame. And I put stuff above the bath. Where do you look when you're in the bath? Straight ahead. Into your subconscious. Into your reality.

JEN. She's had all sorts up there. Sunsets, quotes, pets…

GAVI*'s impressed with her 'commitment'.*

GAVI. Sounds like you'll be an expert with this! So, the daily practice of visualising your dreams as though they're already complete can accelerate your achievement of those / dreams

DAWN *yawns, subtly.*

DAWN. Sorry. Otis was tugging.

GAVI. This practice has given high achievers what seems like super / powers –

JEN. The sofa probably didn't help either.

DAWN. Sorry?

JEN. If you slept in your own bed for once, you might get a good night's sleep.

GAVI *draws attention to the board.*

GAVI. So, what I'm gonna ask you both / to do –

DAWN. What is wrong with you?

JEN. I'm just saying.

DAWN. Well, don't.

Silence.

GAVI.…is just a small visualisation exercise that will / help –

DAWN. Do you know how long I've been with your dad? Twenty-seven years. You couldn't even make it work with Mike for two.

JEN. Least I didn't stay with him out of convenience.

DAWN. It's a marriage! Not some unhealthy, toxic fling.

JEN. And that's what mine was, was it?

DAWN. That's exactly what it was! You were bloody brainwashed!

JEN. *I* ended it, didn't I?

DAWN. Oh come off it Jen. *He* did. Because his wife told him to.

JEN. You're enjoying this, aren't you?

GAVI *(carefully)*. So let's put the 'positive' into / positive visualisation.

DAWN. Gavi, sorry, do you mind if I just have a –

She leaves, clearly struggling.

JEN. Do you remember that time we played *Blind Date* in here? And fat Mark cried 'cause we wouldn't let him be Cilla?

GAVI. Don't you think you should… [go after her.]

JEN. And you chose Lindy as your date 'cause you asked us which Power Ranger we'd be and she said the yellow one, but I'd never seen it so I didn't have a clue what she was on about.

Did you finger Lindy that day?

GAVI *(horrified)*. We were about ten.

JEN. Fat Mark fingered me that day.

GAVI. Are you serious?

JEN. He was sad 'cause he couldn't be Cilla and I was sad 'cause you didn't pick me. Saddest foreplay I've ever had.

She smirks.

GAVI. You shouldn't talk to her like that.

JEN. You don't have to live with her. So, just – [leave it.]

GAVI. She's bound to still have wobbles. Nothing like what happened before though. Surely that's worth celebrating?

JEN. Jesus, how long do we need to keep celebrating it? How's your mum anyway? I mean, she's the one who's *actually* ill.

Sorry. I'm… that sounded – I genuinely want to know how she's doing.

GAVI. She's fine.

JEN. Bet she loves having you back.

GAVI. Love being back.

JEN. Why?

GAVI. It's just home.

JEN. Yeah but Stabbo? It's the only place I know that's named after its knife crime. You had a flat on the seafront.

GAVI. It wasn't on the seafront. It was next to a Greggs and seagulls shat on me weekly. You lot go on about Brighton as though it's Bali.

JEN. It is compared to here.

If I don't get that job, I'm probably just gonna jump off a bridge.

GAVI. Feeling positive then?

JEN. Actually, that's how shit Stabbo is; there's only one bridge high enough to jump off.

GAVI. Why don't you do one of those little concerts again?

She laughs.

JEN. Because I'm not twelve?

GAVI. You absolutely smashed that rendition of 'Row, Row, Row Your Boat'.

She punches him playfully.

JEN. Fuck off! I never played that.

He laughs.

GAVI. Genuinely though. Used to love it. Hearing you and that.

She scoffs.

And doing something like that again, y'know – playing in front of someone, might help with the audition.

JEN. Keyboard's at Mike's, so.

He doesn't push it.

GAVI. Whenever you did one of those concerts –

JEN (*mockingly*). Me singing to like four people in my bedroom – was hardly a 'concert'. Going on like I was at the O2.

GAVI. Performances then, whatever. Whenever you did them, I'd sit there feeling like a bit sick for you, 'cause I could tell how nervous you were. Even though you were the one who'd invited us to come and watch you in the first place. But when you started singing… it was like, none of us were even there. You were just, so…

JEN. Didn't you make me a banner once?

It had like little red hearts around the edge.

GAVI. I mean, they were flames, but whatever.

They smile.

How does it make you feel? Singing? Playing?

JEN. Alright Louis Theroux.

GAVI. I'm serious. I wanna know.

She's uncomfortable but goes with it.

JEN. I dunno. You just get a bit lost in it. Helps to forget other stuff. Sounds pathetic, but.

GAVI. It doesn't. I remember this one night, this was back when we were at school, we'd lost five nil against Bramcote Hills and I was in proper mard about it. My mum was pretty ill at the time and all. Some days, she like, could barely even walk. So what with that and the footie, I was just on a proper downer about it all. Anyway, that night we're about to have our tea and she keeps trying to make me laugh, and nothing's working, I'm just – I'm not budging – and this song comes on the radio, and she turns it up and starts properly getting into it. She's singing into this spatula, which still has this bit of bolognese on it and I keep thinking it's gonna drip on to her top, but she's so into it, she doesn't even notice. And I'm watching her, sort of embarrassed, even though it's just us two. But also, sort of in awe as well. Because, she's just like, lost. Like, she's gone somewhere. Somewhere better. But then she starts playing up to it 'cause I start laughing 'cause it is getting a bit cringe. Head back, eyes closed, bloody bolognese spatula in the air

JEN *smiles.*

JEN. What was the song?

He winces.

Piss off, not that one by Spandau Ballet?

He laughs.

A moment between them.

She jumps up and gets a biscuit.

GAVI. Do you want a brew?

JEN. Have you not got anything else?

GAVI. Club biscuits? But I see you've found those.

JEN. Do you wanna get pissed?

GAVI. It's Wednesday.

JEN. And?

He shakes his head.

She settles for halving her biscuit with him; they eat their biscuits together.

So, just to be sure, definitely didn't finger Lindy in here?

GAVI. No!

JEN. It's mad innit, the stuff you remember. The stuff you *think* you remember.

When we were younger, did you ever think about…

GAVI. What…?

She starts laughing.

JEN. Think about…

GAVI. What?!

JEN.…fingering *me* in here?

He goes to speak but can't.

Alright Gavi, chill out with your boner.

GAVI *is mortified. He starts stacking the chairs.*

I'm only messing!

Beat.

You haven't actually thought / about…

GAVI. No! Bellend.

I really think you should go and check on your mum.

JEN. I thought you were gonna talk to me about – (*Mocking.*) positive visualisation.

GAVI *turns to the page on the flip chart that says, 'Spreading the word!' They don't speak for a moment.*

Why you being weird?

GAVI. I'm not.

JEN. I was only joking.

GAVI. I know! I just really need to get on.

JEN gathers her stuff together and heads to the door.

JEN. You on an early tomorrow?

GAVI. Bright and early.

He starts adding to the list:

'Posters'

'Flyers'

'Leaflets'

'Canvassing'

JEN. Sure you're alright?

GAVI. Yeah!

JEN. Is it 'cause I think Spandau Ballet are shit?

He smirks.

By the way, if I don't get this job in Madrid, I don't have to pledge a hundred quid do I? 'Cause I haven't got a hundred quid, so...

GAVI. Better get the job then.

She leaves. He stops writing – his smile instantly fading. After a moment, he begins to write again.

3

The flip chart reads: 'Week 3 – Go Get It! DRUM ROLL PLEASE!'

GAVI *gestures towards the board.*

DAWN *and* JEN *do a drum roll.*

GAVI. So guys, as you know, for the last few weeks, the turnout's been –

DAWN. Shit.

GAVI. I was going to say minimal, but cheers Dawn. And I've been racking my brain, trying to work out how we get everyone out *there* in *here*. And I've got it!

They stop the drum roll.

Well at least carry on until I actually announce it –

JEN (*gestures to her fingers*). It's actually quite painful –

DAWN. We'll count down instead – five –

> DAWN *and* JEN *count down but it's not in sync. At three,*
> GAVI *can't contain his announcement any longer.*

GAVI. I'm gonna throw a fundraiser!

> *He waits for them to react.*

> Don't get too excited. This isn't just gonna be like, *any*
> fundraiser – this is gonna be an *epic* fundraiser, yeah? Think
> of it as more of an experience rather than an event.

JEN. Has Stapleford ever had a fundraiser?

DAWN. No one will know what to do.

GAVI. An entire day devoted to making our community realise
they can do *anything* if they put their minds to it.

DAWN. How you gonna do that, then?

> GAVI *circles the space.*

GAVI. Picture this. People come in, we welcome them by
giving them some like, green tea…

> *They're not impressed.*

> Or Club biscuits, whatever. And then I stand up and say,
> 'Hands up if you want more from life?'

> DAWN'*s hand shoots up.*

> Exactly! So, everyone will put their hands up. And I'll be
> like, 'Ladies and Gentlemen, you've come to the right place.
> Because here at Go Get It, we are gonna change your lives.
> Right here. Right now.' Shit, I've got goosebumps. Have you
> got goosebumps?

DAWN. Yeah, very goosebumpy.	JEN. Yeah, goosebumps, the lot.

They haven't.

GAVI. And then, I can stand up here – pretend it's a podium.

He stands on a bucket.

And then I'll ask them how they'd like a life that is rich with possibilities, excitement and opportunities –

He steps down.

And then I thought we could present some sort of masterclass. To give them a taste of what to expect when they join the meetings –

DAWN....like a masterclass in positive visualisation?

GAVI. Exactly Dawn! And you can get your little picture-frame family out and tell everyone about that –

JEN. Please don't –

GAVI. – And not only will this be a good opportunity to get more people to come, we can also earn a few extra quid on the side for resources and that!

DAWN. It's not a bad idea actually.

GAVI. We'll do a raffle and a bake sale, and at the end, I'll give everyone a free T-shirt and –

JEN. Will they fit this time?

They all look down at their T-shirts.

GAVI. They are quite roomy, aren't they?

DAWN. They're absolutely massive, Gavi.

GAVI. And then everyone will leave with their free T-shirts, signed up to the meetings and we'll all just be... connected. Inspired. Motivated. BOOM.

JEN. Not being funny or anything, but if no one can be arsed to come to these meetings, why would they come to a fundraiser?

GAVI. Aha! The clue is in the name...

FUNdraiser! Because it'll be fun!

They're not convinced.

Look. People are intrigued by Go Get It... but they don't like committing themselves to stuff. It's the fear of the unknown...

So, all we need to do is give them a glimpse into the unknown and it won't be so unknown any more! They'll sign up, trust me. Dawn, can you be in charge of the bake sale?

DAWN. Me?

JEN. You're good at baking. She'll do it.

DAWN*'s taken aback.*

DAWN. Am I?

JEN (*throw away*). Yeah.

GAVI. So, all good with the baking?

DAWN (*chuffed*). Yep.

GAVI. Jen, if you could be in charge of the decor –

JEN *pulls a face.*

I don't mean chandeliers or anything like that – just something to brighten the place up a bit. Fairy lights or a few banners...

Her face remains.

Or y'know, just turn up.

She agrees.

Brilliant. So, let's still carry on with these meetings, even if it's just to keep momentum and that, and then we do the fundraiser in say, a month? Before Jen gets her big break! Agreed?

DAWN (*mouth full of biscuit*).   JEN. Agreed.
Agreed!

GAVI. This is the way forward, team. For all of us. Those who say 'I can't' and those who say 'I can' are both usually right.

DAWN *gives him a little applause.*

4

The flip chart says: 'Week 4 – Go Get It! SELF DEVELOPMENT!'

DAWN *is standing on a chair. She opens her mouth, but nothing comes out.*

DAWN. Sorry. I get dead nervous with stuff like this.

GAVI. Take your time.

DAWN *takes a deep breath.*

Well, not too much time 'cause we start at seven.

DAWN. Should I stand up here?

GAVI. No.

DAWN. No, okay.

She climbs down.

Good evening, people of Stapleford – / that's quite formal, no, okay.

GAVI. Yeah, no don't say that.

DAWN. Hello. I am very glad you could all join me here at… need to think of a name.

GAVI. We can come back to that.

She centres herself.

DAWN. Have you ever been alone and had a feeling that you *weren't* alone… perhaps you've felt a presence at the bottom of the bed… or seen something in the reflection of the mirror that wasn't you… if so, you may be experiencing a variety of sensations that could be linked to paranormal activity –

GAVI. Not necessarily. My mum heard this story on *The One Show* where this guy thought he had a poltergeist. All sorts of weird shit happened to him. Couldn't get his breath, he kept hearing weird noises, he even started to hallucinate… turns out he had a gas leak.

DAWN. Gavi!

GAVI. Sorry.

DAWN *sits down, deflated.*

Hey, come on –

DAWN. No, I hate public speaking. I can't even talk on the tannoy at work. Once I stuttered so much, a customer thought I was being held at gunpoint.

GAVI. I want you to picture someone who you admire for their public speaking. Someone who's excelled in it.

DAWN. Dermot O'Leary.

GAVI. I was gonna go with Martin Luther King but sure, Dermot it is. Picture him right now speaking… excelling. You've got this.

DAWN *stands back up, encouraged.*

JEN *enters.*

JEN. Why is there a framed picture of Phillip Schofield above the bath?

DAWN. Because I like him.

JEN. I like Stormzy but I'm not gonna frame him in the bog.

DAWN. It's my house and if I want a picture of Phillip Schofield above the bath, then I'll have a picture of Phillip Schofield above the bath.

JEN. And Dad's alright with that is he?

DAWN. He wouldn't even notice if Phillip was in our bed, let alone framed above the bath.

JEN. Why are you calling him Phillip like you know him? Do you actually think looking at a picture of him is going to bring you closer to him?

GAVI. Not being disrespectful or anything Dawn but I don't really think you're his type –

DAWN. You're interrupting my rehearsal.

JEN. Rehearsal for what?

GAVI. Her paranormal evening.

JEN (*to* GAVI). I thought you were rehearsing with me.

DAWN *gestures to the door.*

DAWN. If you could wait outside, we'll be with you shortly.

JEN. Gavi, you said if I was to come before seven, we could do my rehearsal –

DAWN. Well you'll have to wait your turn.

JEN. Gavi, tell her –

DAWN. No, Gavi, tell *her.*

JEN. But I asked him / first.

DAWN. Jen, you cannot get your own way / all the time.

JEN. It's not about getting my own way, / we arranged it last week!

DAWN. Just because your dad says yes to absolutely everything you say.

JEN. At least he listens to me.

DAWN. You never talk to me!

JEN. Because you never listen!

DAWN. Well go on then, I'm listening!

JEN. Great, twenty years too late,

DAWN. Oh, it's all my fault isn't it? It's never yours. You just bloody swan around, thinking / you know everything –

GAVI. Ladies, come on –

JEN. Fuck's sake!

JEN *kicks a bucket.*

This fucking place! Same faces, same complaints, same self-service voice going on and on every bloody minute, whilst everyone stands at their little tills, giving me evils, as if it's *my* fault their pissing bananas haven't registered and I swear to god if anyone else kicks up a fuss about paying five pee for a bag, I'm gonna...

JEN *tries to compose herself.*

DAWN....They're actually ten pee.

JEN. Today this woman asked me where the milk was and next thing I know, she's having a go at me for not smiling at her. And as she went on at me about how customer service isn't what it used to be, I actually fantasised about grabbing her hair and just really aggressively pulling it. To the point where I genuinely thought I was gonna do it.

GAVI. I fantasise about swearing at customers.

JEN. I fantasise about them falling over.

DAWN. I fantasise about putting my fingers into their eye sockets and poking them until they can't see any more.

They stare at DAWN, *who nods to confirm.*

JEN. And Stef is being an absolute bitch.

DAWN. No, come on. Don't go blaming Stef. I shouldn't say anything, it's not my place.

JEN. I couldn't give a shit about what's going on with her, Mum.

DAWN. Her and Dave are getting a divorce.

GAVI. Dawn!

DAWN. Well everyone's going to know at some point! She's being short with everyone. She gave Meera a disciplinary for forgetting her asbestos gloves when she was on freezer duty. Poor woman's got frostbite now. Anyway, Stef's going through a hard time and we all just need to give her some support.

JEN. She ripped your paranormal poster off the wall.

DAWN. She did what?!

JEN. Said it was a load of bollocks.

DAWN. The absolute cow, I'll kill her.

GAVI. Channel this into positive energy!

DAWN. No wonder Dave's bloody divorcing her.

GAVI. You won't even need your posters up soon, people will be fighting over places.

How many people have said they're coming?

DAWN. Two.

GAVI. Apart from me and Jen?

DAWN *refuses to meet his eye.*

There's still time.

DAWN. What's the point?

GAVI *fiddles with his phone and speakers. He plays 'Gold' by Spandau Ballet.*

Christ, not again.

GAVI *places his hands on* DAWN*'s shoulders.*

GAVI. All I want you to do is close your eyes and just…

JEN *watches him.*

GAVI *loses himself in it.* DAWN *doesn't.*

Did you not go anywhere?

DAWN. Where was I meant to have gone?

He shrugs it off.

I know what you mean though. I had a cardigan that used to do that.

GAVI. A cardigan?

DAWN. Used to take me somewhere. Somewhere safe. It was this red woolly cardigan I got from a charity shop. And yeah, it was haunted.

GAVI. Sorry, the cardigan was haunted?

DAWN. Yeah, by its previous owner. No matter how many times I washed it, it still smelt like her – a bit like TCP. And whenever I was having one of my bad days, Otis would curl up in my cardigan, away from all the horrible stuff and everything felt safe.

But when Otis died, the cardigan vanished… It was like Otis took it with him. So, he could carry on feeling safe.

She smiles.

Sometimes, I walk into certain rooms in the house and it's like I can still smell her. The woman who haunted the cardigan.

She ponders, nostalgically.

I've got a feeling the woman's name was Vera. She smelt like a Vera.

GAVI *looks terrified.*

So, don't worry. I don't think you're mad.

GAVI. Oh good. Look, if you're cool with us starting at seven thirty and then me and Jen can rehearse –

JEN. Not really in the mood now.

DAWN *scoffs.*

DAWN. I blame Mike.

JEN *laughs.*

If you hadn't stopped singing in the first place, you might not be needing any rehearsals.

JEN. What's that got to do with Mike?

DAWN. That was your thing – your little spark. And when you moved in with him, it just sort of… went out.

JEN. What are you on about? I'm literally applying for a job to do it!

DAWN. Only to get away from me.

JEN*'s losing the will to live*.

He's never supported you. With anything.

JEN. Yes he has!

DAWN. Why did he make you keep your keyboard in his garage then?

JEN. He didn't *make* me keep it in his –

DAWN. Granddad told us he did. And he's not exactly gonna lie to us, is he?

GAVI (*cautiously*). To be fair, he lied to Nando's.

JEN. He didn't *make* me keep it in his garage, there just wasn't enough space in the house!

DAWN. Bollocks.

JEN. I don't even know why we're having this conversation, it's pointless –

DAWN. I used to love listening to you sing.

JEN. When?! You were never / [there.]

DAWN. For years, I would sit at the top of the stairs. Just listening to you sing in your room. And you sounded so…

It was a part of you – a lovely part of you. And since you've been back, I don't know where that part of you has gone.

JEN. How do you always manage to make me feel even more shit about myself?

DAWN. Me?!

JEN. Stop blaming Mike for everything! You make out that he's this sort of monster –

DAWN. He is! I've see the way he goes about the place.

JEN. It's his job!

DAWN. His *job*? He's a bent copper, not bloody Al Capone.

DAWN*'s alarm goes off.*

JEN*'s at breaking point.*

I'm a busy woman, I need reminding about these things.

GAVI. What's it reminding you about?

JEN. *Emmerdale.*

DAWN *struggles to switch the alarm off.*

The calm after the storm. No one speaks for a moment.

GAVI (*confirming to* DAWN). Dawn. Seven thirty. Please?

DAWN *decides not to rise to it and exits.*

JEN. Do you think I'm tapped? Up here? (*Gestures to her head.*)

GAVI. Why would I think that?

JEN. Genetics? It'd make sense. I feel like shit pretty much every day. And if I do have it, depression or anxiety or whatever, this is it, isn't it? For life. Look at my mum.

GAVI. You've gotta start focusing on the positives Jen, she's much better than she was –

JEN. But it's still a thing isn't it? Still something we have to factor into everything.

GAVI *goes to comfort her but she's too consumed to notice.*

I don't think she's been taking her sweets – Prozac – used to call them sweets. So, she's either stopped taking her sweets, or I dunno, maybe she's right. Maybe it *is* me – maybe *I'm* the reason she's all…

GAVI. Course it's not you –

JEN. – Last night, I was watching *First Dates* and she comes in and starts going on about how Joe Wicks is doing this litter picking event in the Market Square on Saturday and how we should go. I was like, 'No ta.' And then she just starts having a go at me about how I don't wanna do anything any more and I'm like, 'No. I just don't want to go litter picking with Joe Wicks.' And then she's like, 'Well I think you're selfish.' And I'm like 'How? I pick up my own litter, it's not my problem everyone else is a fucking imbecile that they have to rely on Joe Wicks to do it,' and then she just starts crying. And my dad comes in and tells me to stop making it worse, and I'm like – I'm literally just trying to watch *First Dates* in peace and all of a sudden, this is *my* fault? Just because someone's had depression, what – the rest of us are expected to just tiptoe around them forever? If *I* get diagnosed, does that mean I can get away with treating people like shit too? She's still going on and on so I just turn the TV louder to drown her out. I've never put it louder than like, twenty-eight – managed to get it to fifty, which was awful, for everyone. She cried a bit more, told me I'm sending her under again and went to bed.

GAVI. Do you think she *is*… 'going under' again?

JEN. One of us is.

Do you remember those Saturday mornings we'd watch *Ministry of Mayhem* and drink Capri-Suns? Those were the best days of our lives and no one thought to tell us. Feel sort of, conned.

He tries to comfort her.

Anyway. Go on, do your magic.

GAVI. Jen, listen, if you'd rather just talk about –

JEN. Me and my mum being tapped? Nah.

GAVI *shifts, uncomfortably.*

What?

GAVI. 'Tapped.' I don't like it. It's like slang for being… mentally unstable.

JEN. …Yeah, 'cause that's what it is.

He shifts, uncomfortably.

It's just a word, Gavi.

GAVI. But there are kinder words.

JEN (*snaps*). Yeah well, life isn't kind, so.

Can you just help me?

(*Softer.*) Please.

He gently brings her into the centre of the garage and stands opposite her.

GAVI. Remember. Positive up here. Positive out there.

She's not sold.

Let's do some breath work and then we can go through some power poses and visualisation.

So, to centre yourself, close your eyes and...

GAVI *closes his eyes.*

JEN *closes one eye but keeps the other open, watching him.*

Breathe in for four, hold for four, out for four.

He opens his eyes.

What?

She shakes her head.

Breathe in for four, three, two / one

JEN. Why are you doing this?

GAVI. For the diaphragm.

JEN. Why are you doing this for *me*?

GAVI. I want you to achieve your goal.

JEN. Do you actually think I will?

GAVI. Hundred per cent.

They look at one another for a moment.

JEN. If I get this job –

GAVI (*correcting*). *When* I get this job…

JEN. *When* I get this job… do you wanna come?

He's floored.

GAVI. To Madrid?

JEN. You could just come back if it wasn't your thing, or you could get a job there? (*Teases.*) They might have a Co-op.

He smiles.

You could come out whenever, obviously depending on your mum and –

GAVI. Yeah. Yeah, that'd be…

He beams.

I'm just gonna –

He suddenly runs out of the garage.

JEN *stands in the space, unsure of what's happening.*

(*Offstage.*) Close your eyes!

JEN. Why?

GAVI (*offstage*). Just do it!

She does so, reluctantly.

GAVI *enters, carrying a large piece of equipment, disguised beneath a sheet. He places it down in front of her.*

He whips the sheet off to reveal her keyboard.

Okay, you can look!

She opens her eyes.

I thought you could practise properly. I know you don't need to play it in the audition or anything but like I said, thought it could help you get back into the swing of it?

JEN. But – I thought it was at…?

GAVI. Mike's, yeah, but, well – I just thought it would save you having to speak to him again and –

JEN. You went to Mike's?

He nods.

Was he alright?

GAVI. Think so.

JEN. Did he ask about me?

GAVI. Er, yeah?

JEN. What did he say?

GAVI.… 'How's Jen?'

JEN. And what did you say?

GAVI.… 'Fine.'

JEN. Fuck's sake, what do you mean 'Fine'?

GAVI. What's wrong with that?

JEN. You should have said 'great' or 'brilliant'. How would you feel if I spoke to one of your exes and told them you were doing 'fine'?

GAVI.… I'd feel fine.

JEN. Was he nice to you? Like, did he offer you a drink or anything?

GAVI. No.

JEN. Was the house a mess?

GAVI. I dunno.

JEN. What do you mean 'you dunno'?

GAVI. Well I didn't see enough to fully inspect the cleanliness of the place.

JEN. Has she moved her stuff back in?

GAVI. How am I meant to know?

JEN. Well was he alone?

GAVI. I think so.

JEN. You think so?

GAVI. Well I only went in the garage but I dunno, suppose someone could have been in there.

JEN. What makes you say that? Did you hear her?

GAVI. No!

JEN. Well why didn't you go in and – and, have a look round?

GAVI. Because I'm not mental!

Instantly regretting his choice of phrase.

I just asked if I could grab your keyboard because we were practising for this audition, he asked what audition and I said for this bar job in Madrid and then he –

JEN. No you didn't.

GAVI. What?

JEN. You didn't tell him about Madrid.

GAVI. Well… I didn't say what it was *for.*

JEN. You literally just said you said it was for a bar job in Madrid.

Beat.

GAVI. Yeah, but I didn't like, say… what bar.

JEN *grabs her belongings.*

I thought you'd be buzzing!

JEN. You told him.

GAVI. So? He was gonna find out at some point!

JEN. Not from you!

GAVI. Why does it matter? You're not even together!

She heads to the door, upset.

I don't get it Jen.

JEN. You've fucked up. You've really fucked up.

GAVI. But I was just trying to –

JEN. Well, don't.

She exits.

He throws a sheet back over the keyboard – defeated. Again.

5

The flip chart reads: 'Week 5 – Go Get It! DAWN'S PARANORMAL NIGHT!' followed by doodles of ghosts.

DAWN *is putting out various props on the table; a pair of dowsing rods, a jewellery box and a bell.*

GAVI*'s sorting out a load of folders. He's slightly more downbeat than we've seen him.*

DAWN *rings the bell, amused.*

DAWN. Been trying to think of a name for my group but…

GAVI. 'Dawn and the dead'?

She's not impressed.

DAWN. No. Listen, two have signed up! Was actually nearly four. Meera wanted to but she's still got frostbite and Stef wanted to, but she's still a cow.

DAWN*'s alarm goes off.*

Emmerdale can wait!

GAVI *picks up the dowsing rods, studying them.*

Gavi, you mustn't – [touch them.]

GAVI *cautiously hands them over.*

The rods will draw us to the right answer.

GAVI. Right answer to what?

DAWN. Anything.

She goes to demonstrate.

Left for no. Right for yes.

GAVI. Will Dawn's paranormal night be a success?

They watch carefully. The rods roll to the left.

Does left mean…?

DAWN. Left means no.

Beat.

DAWN *checks the time again*

GAVI *looks for a specific folder.*

I've been googling some recipes. For the bake sale.

GAVI. Yeah?

DAWN. Couldn't believe what Jen said. About me being good. Baking's for proper mums.

GAVI. As opposed to what?

DAWN. A mum like me.

GAVI. You are a proper mum.

DAWN. Yeah but look at your mum. She made jam. I always wanted to be a mum that made jam. Every time you had a school fete, I used to feel so bad about not making them, that I'd just buy a batch of Hartley's, rip all the labels off and pass them off as my own.

He laughs.

Does that make me a bad mum?

GAVI. No. A fraud perhaps, but.

DAWN. Jen doesn't think I was a proper mum.

GAVI. Course she does.

Beat.

DAWN. Would your mum be up for tonight? Is it her sort of thing?

GAVI. Not really.

DAWN. How's she / getting on?

GAVI hands over a folder.

GAVI. For you.

Open it.

She does.

DAWN (*reading it*). 'Personal development folder' – very fancy.

GAVI. Good way to keep track of your progress. And there's a checklist in there. To make sure you're pushing yourself out of your comfort zone.

DAWN. Tick…

She holds the page up.

GAVI. You bought a stranger a coffee?

DAWN. They didn't like coffee so I bought them a tea instead.

GAVI. Seriously?

She nods proudly.

DAWN. I was in Costa and I got this feeling that I just had to do it. I got butterflies!

GAVI. Will you make a speech at the fundraiser? Tell them that?

DAWN (*horrified*). What, like public speaking?

GAVI. Think of it as more like chatting in front of friends…

DAWN*'s not sold.*

Have a think.

DAWN *checks the time. Disappointment creeps in.*

Why don't we treat tonight as a practice? And then when
more people have signed up after the fundraiser, you can
hold another?

She's gutted, but goes with it.

DAWN. Turn off the lights.

GAVI. Why?

DAWN. No one contacts spirits with the big light on.

*He apprehensively switches them off, leaving the stage and
audience in darkness.*

GAVI. Dawn?

DAWN. Yeah?

GAVI. Cool.

Beat.

Dawn?

DAWN. Mmm?

GAVI. Nothing.

Beat.

I'm just thinking, shall we –

DAWN. I'm trying to get in the zone, Gavi.

GAVI. Sorry.

Silence.

DAWN. I need you to relax.

A moment.

Are you relaxed?

GAVI. Yep.

He's not.

DAWN. Tonight, we are –

JEN opens the door.

JEN. One condition: I'm not doing a ouija board.

DAWN. Don't have one. Not since your dad used it as a chopping board.

JEN shuts the door; complete darkness again.

(*Sincerely.*) Thanks Jen.

Tonight, we are going to try and contact any spirits that choose to cross our path. We have a few props to help us do this.

The jewellery box begins to play a nursery rhyme tune.

JEN (*quietly*). Oh, fuck off.

DAWN. We also have a bell – (*Demonstrating.*) and some dowsing rods, which we'll use to communicate with the spirits.

GAVI. Did you hear that? I swear I just heard something.

DAWN. Now, there's been sightings in Stapleford of an elderly gentleman that goes by the name of William. He passed over in the late 1800s and according to my research, he had a very 'colourful' life, which may be revealed in tonight's findings. We're now going to try and contact him.

GAVI. Dawn, I've gone really cold.

DAWN. I'd like us to go around and introduce ourselves to William and listen very carefully to his response.

JEN. His response? He's dead, isn't he?

DAWN (*snapping*). Yes Jen. He is. But his spirit lives on. So, whoever he responds to, with a sound or a sign, is the person he wants to communicate with.

She gets in the zone.

Hello William. I'm Dawn. If you could show us a sign that you're with us, we'd really appreciate it.

Silence.

GAVI *(nervously)*. Alright William. I'm um, I'm Gavi. Um. A lot of people when they first meet me call me Gavin, which is a bit annoying, as it is just Gavi. I actually had a Great-Uncle Gavi who apparently lived in Southampton –

DAWN. That'll do love. Jen?

JEN. No chance.

GAVI *gasps.*

GAVI. Shit! I swear I just heard something... like a word.

DAWN. Jen, speak to him again –

JEN. Piss off.

DAWN *and* GAVI *both gasp.*

GAVI. See! Did you hear?   DAWN. Yes I did! I heard
                                 something!

JEN. Sorry, can someone tell me what we're meant to have heard?

GAVI. It sounded like 'roar' or maybe, like, 'whore'.

JEN. Sorry?

DAWN. Gavi, knowing what I know, you could be spot on with that.

JEN. What the fuck is happening?

DAWN. We think William might have called you a 'whore'. Now, it's dead interesting that William's hostile response was to Jen, especially with how hostile she was towards him.

JEN. *Him?* He's a corpse! He doesn't exist!

DAWN. It could be a response to hearing a young female voice... which would make sense. Knowing what I know.

GAVI. Oh my god, what do you know?

DAWN. William had a fondness for young, pretty women.
He was known in the town for having his way with them.

JEN. Wonder if he knows fat Mark. They'd have loads in
common.

GAVI. Dawn, I need to get out of here. My heart's like…

DAWN. You're okay, you're alright –

GAVI. No, I don't think I am you know – wait, are you behind
me?

DAWN. No, I'm here – to your left.

GAVI. Who's that breathing then?

JEN. Hopefully all of us.

GAVI. Someone's breathing right on my neck! Shit! Dawn,
I need to get out, like now, quick! Please!

DAWN. Try and calm down Gavi –

GAVI. Please, turn the light on – turn the light on!

Suddenly, there's a loud knock on the door. They all scream.

DAWN. Okay, it's okay. (*Calls out.*) You're too late I'm afraid,
we've already started!

VOICE. Police! Open up!

JEN. Mike?

DAWN. *Your* Mike?

Another loud knock.

VOICE. Open up!

GAVI. Ignore it, he'll go away.

DAWN. He won't –

JEN (*calls out*). Mike?

DAWN (*hushed*). Jen!

GAVI. Just leave it –

JEN (*calling out*). Hold on, one minute –

JEN *goes to answer the door.*

DAWN. Jen! Just hang on and let me deal with –

JEN *opens the door.*

ACT TWO

6

The flip chart reads: 'Week 6 – Go Get It! FUNDRAISER
PREP: FAIL TO PREPARE, PREPARE TO FAIL!'

Fundraiser preparation is in full flow. GAVI *is decorating*
a poster. DAWN *is draping fairy lights around the place.*
She switches them on, followed by a little reveal celebration.

She gestures to the lights.

DAWN. Aldi. It's got everything that place. You go in for a loaf
and you come out with a camping tent.

GAVI *smiles, appreciating her efforts.*

Oh! I've also got you a little present…

She goes to her bag but her phone rings, distracting her.
She cancels the call and puts it back in her pocket.

Still not ready to talk to him.

She goes back to search through her bag but keeps getting
distracted by what she's saying.

GAVI. Do you want to talk about it?

DAWN. Not ready for that either.

GAVI. Well, when / you are –

DAWN. He's such a selfish man. To actually lie, when the
man's got more than enough money to pay for his meals.
Slug and Lettuce, fine. Prezzo, fine. But Carluccio's?

And for Mike, of all people, to turn up with him. I don't know
what's worse – him getting his hands on my dad, or Jen.

This stings for both of them.

My dad doesn't give a shit about ruining my paranormal night.

GAVI. I'm sure / he –

DAWN. The only one who believes in me is you. And maybe the man at Costa would.

GAVI's confused.

The one I bought the tea for. Keep seeing him about. If you squint, he looks a bit like Phillip Schofield.

Sometimes he smiles at me. And it's not like a – (*A fake smile.*) but more of a – (*A sort of suggestive smile.*) Makes me feel all...

Anyway. It's not like I'm gonna do anything about it.

GAVI. Why?

DAWN. Gavi, you can't just walk out on twenty-seven years.

GAVI. If you're not happy, *do* something.

DAWN (*quietly*). I've got that on a fridge magnet too.

She tries to lighten the mood. She continues, putting up bunting but again, gets distracted by what she's saying.

When I was *really* ill, when things were at their worst, Stu held everything together. I don't really know how he did it. To get up every day and hold the fort like that, knowing that the person you love feels so much worse about being here, than not being here.

Yeah, not sure how he managed that bit.

And I've not forgotten that. But over time, things do just fade. And now, he never wants to go anywhere or do anything new. We wake up, go to work, come home, wake up, go to work, come home... and it's not as simple as not loving each other any more. But now, it's the sort of love that – if anything happened to either of us, we'd just carry on without the other. And practically speaking, I know that's a good thing, but... not exactly romantic, is it?

He offers a Club biscuit. She declines.

After my mum died, my dad couldn't bear being in the house on his own at night. In the day, he'd keep busy – the practical side of death, he – *we* dealt with. But it was the emptiness… So, every night, he'd put his big coat on, take his radio, his quilt and a glass of something – whiskey usually – and sleep in his shed. He'd go to sleep listening to the radio, 'cause he hated the silence. He did that for weeks, months even.

She tries not to cry.

And I was driving home one night, thinking about it all and I just had this horrible realisation. About Stu. And Jen. That when my time was up, neither of them would need to do any of that. They'd never need to sleep in a shed for me.

GAVI. Course they would.

DAWN. I mean, we don't even have a shed. More of a shit porch, but.

GAVI comforts her.

She changes her mind about the Club biscuit. He leans his head on her shoulder, whilst she eats it.

I really want *you* to meet someone.

He shrugs it off.

Y'know Leah – Stef's daughter – loves the planet – had a go at Stef for drinking a bottle of Evian –

GAVI. Evian Leah?

DAWN. Evian Leah, yeah. She asked me how long you were back for…

GAVI. I'd rather just concentrate on the fundraiser. Speaking of which… thoughts?

He holds up a vibrantly decorated poster saying; 'GO GET IT! NO EXCUSES. SIGN UP NOW!'

DAWN. It's quite aggressive.

Too engrossed to care, he turns the flip chart to a page that says, 'FUNDRAISER TO DO LIST!'

'Decor'

'Baking (Dawn)'

'Raffle prizes – get them'

'Facebook event – update with pics'

'Twitter page – make one'

'Local press'

'Confirm times with Daryl at Notts Post'

'Notts TV?'

'BBC Radio Notts?'

'Billboard?'

'Council?'

'Leaflets?'

'Call McVities – beg for deal'

'Get more chairs'

'Get T-shirts that fit'

'Fix garden gate'

'New kettle?'

'Buy tea and coffee'

'Borrow better speakers'

'Motivational quotes for each wall'

'Make poster for outside'

'Make poster for inside'

'Make poster for Co-op'

'Design logo'

'Quiz?'

~~*'Bunting'*~~

'Guest speaker? Dawn?'

DAWN *spots the list.*

Bloody hell. Lots to do in less than two weeks.

GAVI. Still struggling with the raffle prizes.

DAWN. Would your mum be up for making some of her jam? Or is that not –

He shakes his head.

How is she?

GAVI. She'll be alright.

DAWN. Stef did say she'd popped round yesterday, but didn't manage to…

GAVI. We were at a check-up.

DAWN. Listen, if there's anything we / can do –

GAVI. Have you seen Jen at all since – ?

DAWN *shakes her head.*

When you do, can you tell her the rehearsal offer still stands? I know her audition's on Monday and –

DAWN. – Can I say something? Just between us?

I'm her mum. And I'm telling you, you can do better.

Beat.

Well, once you've had a shower.

He avoids looking at her.

GAVI. It's on my list.

DAWN. Gavi, if you're struggling –

GAVI. I'm fine!

DAWN. When I felt bad, I sometimes went days without. Weeks, even.

GAVI. Dawn, I'm fine! *Fixing* it – fixing the shower is on my list.

DAWN. I've told you, Stu can pop round and do it?

GAVI. Nah, I'll just YouTube it.

DAWN. Don't be daft!

GAVI. I'm skint, so.

DAWN. He won't want paying –

GAVI. We're a bit all over the shop at the minute so –

DAWN. Leave him a key!

GAVI. Taking the piss considering I've not seen him in about ten years.

DAWN. Gavi, he will fix it. End of.

GAVI *relucantly accepts.*

I know that you're busy with the fundraiser, and it really is shaping up to be… (*Searches.*)

GAVI. Epic.

DAWN. Epic, yeah. But stop forgetting about you.

GAVI. I'm not!

DAWN. You are love, you stink.

It's playful between them, despite the concern.

GAVI. What's this present you've got me then?

DAWN *suddenly remembers, goes to her bag and pulls out a packet of Club biscuits with a ribbon tied around them.*

DAWN. Happy first term.

He's really touched.

GAVI. Cheers.

DAWN. Six weeks! What have you got lined up for the next term?

GAVI. …Haven't thought beyond the fundraiser yet. Pass us a bit more of that bunting, will you?

DAWN goes to get more bunting out of a bag, yawning. She passes it to him and he pins it up around the garage.

Otis tugging?

DAWN. I wish. Hilary woke me up at the crack of dawn. All for a Lemsip. To be fair, she is quite ill. She's got this flu she can't seem to / shake –

GAVI. Lemsip won't help.

DAWN. Well, it probably *will* help –

GAVI. Course it won't! All that stuff is up here.

He taps his head.

DAWN. …Sometimes people need a bit more than just up there –

GAVI. – This – (*Taps his head.*) has the ability to cure some crazy shit. Look at you. You didn't need any Lemsips!

DAWN. I had depression, Gavi, not the flu.

GAVI. Yeah but look – you're here, fighting fit, alive to tell the story. *You* did that.

She looks at him for a moment.

DAWN. I needed a lot more than 'up here'.

GAVI. Are you thinking of doing a carrot cake for the bake sale? I reckon it's best not to do anything with nuts – what with allergies. Don't want that hanging over us.

GAVI turns the page and begins to write motivational quotes, one after the other:

'*Push yourself. Because no one else is going to do it for you.*'

'*If you continue to think the way you've always thought, you'll continue to get what you've always got.*'

'*Surround yourself with people who are only going to lift you higher.*'

'*The best way to predict the future is to create it.*'

DAWN *sees how lost he is in what he's doing.*

He continues to write. And write. And write.

She watches him, unsettled.

7

A few days later.

The garage has had a fundraiser makeover. GAVI*'s clearly had very little sleep.*

He puts up the remaining bunting, motivational banners and posters.

He counts down through the fundraiser to-do list. Every single thing is ticked off apart from 'Raffle prizes'.

He turns off the light and switches on the fairy lights. Despite it looking 'epic' the completion is daunting.

He sits down, trying to relax but fails.

8

The flip chart reads: 'Week 7 – Go Get It! LEADERSHI–'
Before GAVI finishes writing, JEN enters.

JEN. Alright.

He's clearly pleased to see her.

GAVI. Alright.

JEN takes in his efforts.

JEN. Bloody hell...

They look at another for a moment. GAVI seems a bit flustered.

GAVI. How have you been? I was thinking about you – on Monday, not you as in *you* – you, as in the audition and, and I was just wondering how you were getting on and –

JEN. I'm going to Madrid.

GAVI. Seriously?

She nods, really pleased.

He's genuinely made up for her.

Shut up! What's congratulations in Spanish?

JEN. ...Las congrats?

GAVI. Well come here then!

He hugs her.

Madrid Jen! Madrid! Which, by the way, if the offer / still stands –

JEN. Mike's gonna come with me.

She pulls away from him.

I should never have had a go at you like that. Should never have blamed you for fucking it up. If anything, you sort of did the opposite.

GAVI. Did I?

JEN. Made him realise I've always been there. And the idea of me not being there…

GAVI. His wife alright with that?

She's caught off guard slightly.

JEN. She's left him. For good, so.

Gavi –

GAVI. Listen, we should celebrate! I'll just have a quick look to see if we've got any…

He exits.

JEN goes to sit down at the keyboard. She takes the sheet off but doesn't play.

DAWN enters with a carrier bag. She gets some dried lavender out of the bag and starts sprinkling it around the garage.

DAWN. In case you were wondering –

JEN. I wasn't –

DAWN. – I'm cleansing the bad energy.

JEN. Think it'll take more than potpourri.

DAWN. It's *lavender.*

Would have been good of you to let us know where you've been hiding.

JEN tinkers with the keys.

I assume you've been at his?

GAVI walks in holding a bottle of prosecco and a collection of mugs.

DAWN continues to sprinkle lavender.

GAVI. Is something burning?

DAWN. I'm just healing the bad energy.

GAVI. No such thing Dawn.

She gestures to the bottle of prosecco.

DAWN. What's the occasion?

GAVI *looks at* JEN – *unable to know if* DAWN *knows yet, he plays it safe.*

GAVI. Week seven!

DAWN. Feels longer than that.

He's noticeably not as 'on it'.

GAVI. Right, well, everything's pretty much set for the fundraiser. Twenty-four people on the Facebook page have said they're coming. Only issue is all I've got for raffle prizes are Club biscuits, so if anyone does have anything to donate from now until Saturday, that'd be great.

DAWN. I've got a voucher for Las Iguanas? If my dad's not tarnished our reputation with them and all.

JEN. You can have my car if you want.

DAWN. What?

GAVI. Your *car*?

DAWN. You want to donate your car to a shitty raffle?

GAVI (*stung*). Alright Dawn.

JEN. Won't need it in Madrid, will I?

DAWN. You've not even had the audition yet!

GAVI. It was on Monday.

DAWN. Monday just gone?

Beat.

The enormity of it sinks in for DAWN.

What, so, you're going?

JEN. Yep.

DAWN *tries to digest it.*

'Well done Jen, I'm really proud of you.'

DAWN. It's a big decision. I just – I don't want you to get ahead of yourself.

JEN. …Positive visualisation.

DAWN. Oh, come off it.

JEN. 'Come off it'? I thought you swore by all that shit?

DAWN. Giving away your car! You're taking it too far.

JEN. *I'm* taking it too far? You're the one who has a photo of Phillip Schofield above the bath.

DAWN. I'm fully aware that's not going to actually draw me closer to him.

JEN. What the fuck is he doing up there then?

DAWN. …You're not donating your car to the raffle.

JEN. Gavi, I'm donating my car to the raffle.

DAWN. Has Mike got anything to do with this?

JEN *laughs in disbelief.*

JEN. You just cannot let things go, can you?

DAWN. I wish I could. I wish I could happily let him go.

GAVI. Well it's your lucky day Dawn, because when she goes to Madrid, he's going with her!

He pops the prosecco open. They both glare at GAVI. *He starts pouring the drink into mugs.*

Couldn't find any glasses so is everyone okay with Fifa '98 mugs?

DAWN. Is that a joke?

JEN. Look. I know in the past, he's been… but he's –

DAWN. Changed?

JEN. He could have arrested Granddad that night. Fourth warnings don't exactly exist, do they?

DAWN. And how do you think *he* feels, eh?

She gestures to GAVI.

He finishes pouring and hands out the mugs. No one takes them.

GAVI. What?

JEN. He's happy for me. Aren't you?

GAVI. Buzzing.

GAVI *gulps his mug of prosecco.*

DAWN. You're so wrapped up in yourself, you can't see how miserable he's been. How much you're holding him back / can you?

GAVI. Whoa, / what?

DAWN. No one's turning up to his sessions, he can't afford prizes for his raffle… he's turned down a date with Leah.

GAVI. Wow.

JEN. Evian Leah?

DAWN. Yes, Evian Leah.

JEN. You can't blame me for that!

DAWN. I can and I will.

JEN. You can't face up to your own problems, so you bury your head in / everyone else's.

DAWN. I actually am facing up to my own problems / thank you.

JEN. Why have you stayed then? Why haven't you left?

DAWN *refuses to answer.*

If you're really that unhappy with Dad, why? Why can't you just leave?

DAWN. Because.

JEN. Go on.

DAWN *struggles*.

DAWN. I'd lose you and all.

JEN. That happened a long time ago.

JEN *zips up her jacket and goes to leave*.

DAWN. Go on then, run away when things get a bit hard, like you / always do.

JEN. You never had any plasters.

DAWN. What?

JEN. When I fell over, you used loo roll. Loo roll on a cut? Whenever I had a bump, you rubbed butter on me.

JEN *gets upset*.

You couldn't even plait my hair.

DAWN. Jen, I was *ill*.

JEN. I know there's no rule book on being a mum but where were you learning from?

This stings.

GAVI. Seriously?

JEN. Go on Gavi, sit on the fence like you always do because you daren't have your own opinions in case, god forbid, you upset / anyone –

DAWN. Pack it in.

JEN. I thought it was something we could grow out of, a rough patch, but years down the line and still, here we are. I mean, nothing's ever gonna change is it? I thought eventually, it'd – we'd get better, but if anything, we've only got worse. I just, I don't... I don't get you.

DAWN. I don't get you either.

JEN. Well you should! You're the mum! I didn't ask to be here, did I? You made that choice, so go on, lead the way. Show me what to do 'cause I clearly haven't got a fucking clue.

DAWN. Nobody's got a clue!

JEN. No but they do Mum, they do!

DAWN. I really did try.

JEN. Did you? You were in bed for most of what I remember.

DAWN. Depression paralyses you Jen. And no matter how much you try to pull yourself out of it, sometimes, you simply can't even lift your head off the pissing pillow, let alone look after a family. Do you not think I *wanted* to be there, watching your assemblies? Watching your concerts? Watching *you*. I wanted to *so* much. But I couldn't. I couldn't. And no one understood. Not properly. People would go, 'Oh but you *look* fine?' or 'I really miss the old you' and I'd be like, 'Do you not think I really miss me too?'

DAWN struggles to speak. JEN doesn't look up.

There were times where I genuinely believed I'd never feel happy again. And the guilt that comes with that, as a mum – as *your* mum… the guilt that I wasn't happy and everyone just kept telling me I should have been. I know I should have been. Because not everyone's bloody scrapbooks come true.

DAWN gathers herself.

And my mum used to put butter on *my* bumps. So that's a generation thing. Not a… a bad mum thing.

Beat.

JEN. Why have you never told me any of that?

DAWN struggles to find a response. She doesn't know.

DAWN. Maybe I didn't think it was fair to try and make you understand it.

JEN. Pretty sure you've passed it on to me, so looks like I will understand it after all.

DAWN. For god's sake Jen, you're not depressed. You're just in love with an absolute twat.

JEN. I am finally trying to make a go of things and you're *still* not happy.

DAWN. With *him*. It doesn't count. He's controlling and manipulative and –

JEN. I actually don't care what you think.

DAWN. Well, you *should* care about what I think! Other daughters would.

JEN. Well I'm clearly not like other daughters.

DAWN. And I'm clearly not like other mums.

JEN. God, I wish you were.

DAWN. You know, you really are a spiteful bitch / when you –

GAVI. Sorry but um… if you want to carry on your argument, by all means, do. But I sort of really need you both to fuck off.

They're really taken aback.

I've um, I've just got a lot going on. And I've sort of carried on with all of this for you two. Basically. The chairs, the T-shirts, the biscuits. Which is fine… but it's been a complete waste of time, hasn't it?

DAWN. No! Not / at –

GAVI. No, no it has. It's been worse than a waste of time, actually. It's been an awakening. A fucking horrible awakening. That what I hoped wouldn't be true, sort of is. And um. I don't want to do this any more. Which is shit because this was the only thing. This was the only thing that was sort of making everything else okay. Which is ridiculous because everything else isn't okay. At all, actually. Everything is, um.

He struggles to hold it together.

JEN. Gavi –

GAVI. So, forget the fundraiser. Forget the meetings.

GAVI *goes to leave.*

Every morning, every evening, you know that the other one will be there. And it's like, you see that as a bad thing. And I tried, I really did. I tried to make you realise that there's more, but I've failed. And I've not just failed at convincing you, I've somehow managed to 'un-convince' me.

He goes to leave again but changes his mind.

Actually, no, you've done that. Yeah, you've done that. And I really don't like either of you, for that. (*To* JEN.) I mean, why are you even here? You hate these sessions.

JEN *is startled.*

JEN. No, / I –

GAVI. If I had what you had… you need to learn some respect for her – (*Gestures to* DAWN.) 'cause she is your mum. And she survived. She is alive and well and… here. So yeah that's my opinion, which I do dare to share, thanks. Although 'god forbid' probably *has* upset you. But I don't care. I actually don't care if I've upset you. Which is pretty sad really, considering the fact that I have cared about you for…

He clears his throat, starting again.

You can keep the T-shirts. If you want. For like… decorating, or…

He leaves.

DAWN *goes to follow him.*

JEN. Mum.

DAWN. We can't leave him like that?

JEN. Just – give him…

DAWN *lingers by the door, unsure as to what to do. They don't speak for a moment.*

DAWN. You're not going to turn into me.

JEN. It's worse. I've turned into me.

DAWN *nods.*

Well, don't nod.

DAWN. I will nod. You're not... very nice, Jen.

If it's any consolation, you were.

JEN *sits with this.*

How long do you think we leave him for?

JEN *doesn't know.*

Will you stay with us tonight?

Please?

JEN *nods.*

DAWN *goes to leave. She turns out the lights. There's a thumping sound.*

JEN. Shit.

DAWN. What was that?

JEN. Tripped over that bloody bucket.

JEN *winces.*

That actually really hurt.

DAWN. Come on. We'll get some butter on it when we get home.

9

The day of the fundraiser. A few days later.

Between them, DAWN *and* JEN *take everything down, removing all of* GAVI*'s work.*

JEN *is trying to open another box.* DAWN *chucks her keys over to help open it.* JEN *slices the box open and pulls out a new Go Get It T-shirt. They're still massive. She places it back in the box.*

Just before she chucks the keys back, she notices the image on the keyring. She holds it up.

JEN. Schofield – on your keys?

>   DAWN *ignores her.*

>   (*Sincerely.*) I'm not being… but, do you *actually* believe the universe is guiding you towards him?

>   *Beat.*

DAWN. It's worked with the man in Costa.

JEN. What man in Costa?

DAWN. Just keep seeing a man in Costa that looks a bit like him.

>   JEN *rolls her eyes.*

>   Roll your eyes all you like but –

>   *She holds up the piece of paper that says 'Jen – Goals – Madrid!'*

>   You're living proof.

JEN. What, so, you're just going to run off with the man at Costa?

DAWN. No, I'm not going to run off with the man at Costa.

>   JEN *roots through another box.*

>   I *am* proud of you. I'm just getting my head round it all.

JEN *doesn't look up.*

And for what it's worth, I knew you'd get the job. I knew it. In here. (*Gestures to her heart.*)

JEN. What do you think we do with these?

She roots through a box of folders.

DAWN. He just said to chuck everything.

JEN. As if he's individually labelled them for people.

DAWN. He hasn't...

JEN *shows her.*

JEN. I didn't get the job.

DAWN. What?

JEN. Seems a bit harsh chucking them. Waste of trees. Are folders made from trees?

DAWN. You didn't get it?

JEN. I didn't go to the audition, so.

DAWN. What do you mean you didn't go?

JEN. Maybe we should just give them to people. Make them feel bad about not coming.

DAWN. Why would you not go?

Jen?

JEN. It's not a big thing. I'm still going to Madrid – just not for the job.

DAWN *struggles to find the words.*

DAWN. Why would you not go for the job? You had an opportunity to actually do something with your life and...

JEN. Stop being dramatic, I'm still going aren't I?

DAWN. For a holiday – it's not exactly the same.

JEN. We're not going on holiday, we're going for good.

DAWN *laughs in disbelief.*

You didn't even remember that it was my audition so don't act as though you care –

DAWN. Jen, I've got a very / busy head at the minute.

JEN. Busy head, yep. Haven't we all.

DAWN. Know what the sad thing is? I think you'd have got it. And I think you'd have been brilliant.

JEN (*snaps*). Mum, if I haven't even got the fucking balls to sing for an audition, how am I meant to do it as a job?

DAWN. Did you even try?

JEN *takes down the posters and places them into a pile.*

Does Mike get it? Jen?

Jen?

JEN. Get what?

DAWN. Your singing. Does he get it? How much it means.

JEN (*snaps*). He's not very musical.

DAWN. I'm not asking if he's in the bloody *Lion King*, I'm asking if he understands.

JEN *puts the folders into a bag and pops it by the door.*

DAWN *watches her, sadly.*

Look. I know I've not been very good at this. (*Gestures to the two of them.*) And I know I've got bits of it wrong. And so have you. But I think that's okay, because we've got some bits of it right.

Haven't we?

JEN (*quietly*). Yeah.

DAWN. What I'm saying – what I'm trying to say, is – we're not even here for very long – not when you think about it. And I don't want us to keep doing this. Because, actually, I'm starting to think we might be the lucky ones.

JEN (*quietly*). How do you figure that out?

DAWN. I don't think Gavi's okay, Jen.

Last night, your dad went to fix his shower. Said the house was a state. Washing up piled high, bins hadn't been taken out, stunk of damp. When he was leaving, he got talking to next door and they said Gavi's mum had been taken to hospital a few weeks ago.

JEN. I thought you knew she'd gone in.

DAWN. I didn't know she was *still* in.

JEN. She's always been in and out. Mum, they're curtain twitchers round here. They love a gossip –

DAWN. This is your dad, Jen. And he's not exactly one for dramatic endings, is he?

JEN sits with this.

When he was telling me about it, he seemed...

DAWN struggles to put it into words.

JEN. Look, when Gavi turns up, we'll talk to him. Make sure everything's okay.

DAWN. But what if he doesn't turn up? I mean, he's barely speaking to us. Could be waiting forever.

JEN shrugs.

JEN. Where else have we got to be?

Fair point.

A silent pact is made to wait for him until he returns.

They try to continue with their task but they give up, unable to concentrate.

Not sure how long they'll be waiting...

DAWN. Don't laugh, but... shall I plait your hair?

I YouTubed it.

JEN *nods, subtly.*

DAWN *stands behind her tentatively.*

I'll just do one. Two's a bit much.

Don't want to run before I can walk.

She begins to plait JEN*'s hair.*

Not pulling, am I?

JEN *shakes her head.*

Neither of them speak for a moment. DAWN *concentrates.*

If at first, you don't succeed, try and try again…

JEN *silently cries.*

I've got that on a fridge magnet.

JEN. How big's your fucking fridge?

10

Winter

The garage is in its original state pre-Go Get It groups. There's still a table, a few stacked chairs and JEN*'s keyboard remains under a dust sheet. The white board and kettle have been shoved to the side, and there's no more Club biscuits to be seen.*

GAVI *enters, holding a duvet, a pillow and a glass of water. He takes his shoes off, zips his coat up and lies down on the ground, beneath his quilt. He plays some music through his phone and closes his eyes.*

11

A few nights later.

GAVI's *in the same spot.* DAWN *and* JEN *quietly enter – they have quilts and pillows too. They settle down next to him. He doesn't stir.*

12

A few weeks later.

GAVI *enters, smartly dressed. He goes to pick up a few bottles of prosecco from one of the boxes but sits down instead. He takes a minute.*

JEN *enters, also smartly dressed and carrying her bag.*

JEN. Did you want a minute, or…?

GAVI *shakes his head.*

She gestures to the bottles.

More pissed everyone is, the better.

GAVI. Sorry, I've hardly had a chance to say hello –

JEN. – Don't be a – don't worry about that.

Neither of them know what to say.

Nice that Leah's here.

Saw she'd 'grammed you both at Nandos.

He nods. She nods. For a bit too long.

…How was it?

GAVI. What, the food or…?

JEN. Yeah. What, what did you… have?

GAVI. Um. Butterfly breast. Chips. Macho peas.

JEN. Which spice?

GAVI. Mango and lime.

JEN. Obvs.

GAVI. Obvs.

Beat.

JEN. And, Leah? She's…?

GAVI *nods, vaguely.*

You didn't drink a bottle of Evian in front of her, did you?

GAVI. She's just trying to save the planet.

JEN. Yet she took you to Nando's. What did she have – air?

GAVI. Mushroom and halloumi burger.

JEN (*under her breath*). Course she fucking did.

GAVI. It wasn't like… that. Just needed to get out.

JEN.…I'd have taken you.

GAVI. Didn't think Mike would have appreciated that.

JEN. Think that's sort of – done.

GAVI *seems slightly surprised.*

GAVI. Are you alright?

She nods. Ish.

What about Madrid?

JEN. Might be going interrailing with Granddad instead.

GAVI. Interrailing with Jim? At seventy-five?

JEN. Said he's been wanting to do it for years.

GAVI. Fair play.

JEN. He's gone and made a bucket list for it. Slightly concerned as Berlin Marathon's on it but.

GAVI. Actually, think of all those free meals.

She smiles.

JEN. Stef just said you might be on the move too…

GAVI. So much for staff confidentiality.

JEN. To be fair, she's had a Baileys.

GAVI. Manager position at the Leicester branch.

JEN. …Are you gonna take it?

GAVI shrugs.

I don't think you should.

You drummed it into us about pushing each other out of our comfort zones and… and that you were gonna change things round here, and… and…

GAVI. And I didn't.

JEN. And now you're just gonna run away to Leicester.

GAVI. I'm not running away –

JEN. – I'd understand if it was a Co-op in like, LA. But Leicester? I mean, that's just down the road. It's hardly gonna be a groundbreaking new chapter for you.

GAVI. I don't want a groundbreaking new chapter.

JEN. No. Sorry.

Silence.

GAVI. Anyway, I'd better…

He gestures to the prosecco bottles.

JEN. I know I'm probably gonna regret this. But can you just sit down for a sec?

Beat.

I really need you to sit down. Before I bottle it. Please. And don't look at me.

GAVI sits on a chair, extremely apprehensive.

And afterwards, I don't want to talk about it.

JEN sits at the keyboard and takes out a scrunched-up piece of paper from her bag, which has the basic chords to 'Gold' by Spandau Ballet on it. She smooths it out, placing it in front of her.

She begins to play few notes. She seems really nervous.

She starts playing 'Gold'. It's softer and slower than the original version.

Stop looking at me then.

She starts to sing the song. Despite her nerves, it's beautiful and gentle.

They don't speak for a moment.

Was thinking of like, getting you something for your mum, well, not *for* your – more, as like a gift to… remember her, but… you don't need a gift to do that – 'cause she's your mum. So, you'll always remember her. Always, so.

Still can't stand the fucking song.

She smiles at him.

He's clearly choked.

GAVI. Thanks Jen.

Thank you.

She reaches into her bag and brings out a red, woolly cardigan.

JEN. I know it sounds tapped but there is something about it that makes you feel safe.

She hands it to him.

GAVI. Does your mum know you've got this?

JEN. Obviously not.

Take it. It does help. In a really weird way.

GAVI. No…

JEN. Honestly, take it.

GAVI. I can't.

JEN. You can.

GAVI. No, it's –

JEN. Please take it –

GAVI. I don't want it Jen, it stinks.

No wonder she kept smelling Vera around if she smelt like this.

She laughs.

Really appreciate it though.

There's a moment between them. She kisses him. It's extremely delicate.

DAWN *enters, also dressed smartly. They immediately break their stance.* JEN *hides the cardigan behind the chair.*

DAWN. Sorry. Hilary started serenading me in the kitchen. So, I just need a minute.

DAWN *goes to sit on the other side of* GAVI. *She takes his hand. The three of them sit in silence for a moment.*

Meera's just asked if she can book on to one of my paranormal nights.

JEN. You gonna do another then?

DAWN *scrunches up her face.*

DAWN. I feel like I've lost it. My gift. And the tugging's stopped. After Otis died, I kept finding empty Sheba cans in the recycling, even though we hadn't bought any in months. It's just things like that that have sort of… it's like a light's gone out.

She playfully nudges GAVI.

Could do with one of your talks.

JEN. Mum's making my dad do them tasks to get him out of his comfort zone. Came home the other night to her feeding him an olive.

DAWN. He's really scared of them.

GAVI (*baffled*). Stu's scared of olives?

DAWN. Petrified.

GAVI. And, what, he ate one?

DAWN. Yeah!

JEN. But the fuss he made. It was like a bush tucker trial.

He's moving out for a bit.

GAVI. Stu is?

DAWN. Not for good, or anything. I just… I thought it might be good to have some time away. You know, from what we know. So, he's going to stay at my dad's for a bit. See how we get on.

It's weird. As soon as we agreed to it, I missed him a bit. And he's not even gone yet.

GAVI *holds her hand.*

GAVI. I think I'd better – [head back in.]

DAWN. I was just telling a few people about Go Get It, y'know, what with the free T-shirts and the biscuits and that… Anyway, I've left a list on your fridge of people who want to come to the next one and there's about eleven.

He's in shock.

GAVI. Eleven?

DAWN. And I've decided that if you do take this job in Leicester –

GAVI. Oh good, you know too –

DAWN. – I'm gonna run the Go Get It meetings.

JEN. You?

DAWN. Yes. Me.

JEN. You can't even talk on the tannoy. How are you gonna talk in front of eleven people?

DAWN. I just did alright in there. Dermot must be doing the trick.

GAVI. Dawn, it's sort of my thing.

DAWN. Well, you should probably stay then.

He struggles.

GAVI. I don't really know what I'm gonna do.

DAWN. You're gonna come and stay with us.

He's overwhelmed by how much he needs to hear this.

GAVI. Okay.

He gets up and heads to the door, taking the prosecco bottles with him. JEN *follows him.*

JEN. Mum?

DAWN. I'll be in in a minute.

JEN and GAVI leave, closing the door behind them.

DAWN stands up, takes a deep breath, closes her eyes and waits…

Is there anyone there? Show me a sign, a noise, anything…? Anything at all?

She opens her eyes and closes them again.

(*Desperate.*) Please.

Disappointed, she goes to walk out but, on her way, she stops.

She sniffs. She turns around, spotting the red cardigan on the floor behind one of the chairs.

She picks it up, clutches it to her chest. Relief doesn't cut it.

Thank you Vera. Thank you.

DAWN *turns out the lights and shuts the door behind her.*

End.

A Nick Hern Book

Tapped first published as a paperback original in Great Britain in 2022 by Nick Hern Books Limited, The Glasshouse, 49a Goldhawk Road, London W12 8QP, in association with Bethany Cooper Productions and Theatre503

Tapped copyright © 2022 Katie Redford

Katie Redford has asserted her right to be identified as the author of this work

Cover image: Madison Coby

Designed and typeset by Nick Hern Books, London
Printed in the UK by Mimeo Ltd, Huntingdon, Cambridgeshire PE29 6XX

A CIP catalogue record for this book is available from the British Library

ISBN   978 1 83904 077 1

Amateur Performing Rights   Applications for performance, including readings and excerpts, by amateurs in the English language throughout the world should be addressed to the Performing Rights Manager, Nick Hern Books, The Glasshouse, 49a Goldhawk Road, London W12 8QP, *tel* +44 (0)20 8749 4953, *email* rights@nickhernbooks.co.uk, except as follows:

Australia: ORiGiN Theatrical, Level 1, 213 Clarence Street, Sydney NSW 2000, *tel* +61 (2) 8514 5201, *email* enquiries@originmusic.com.au, *web* www.origintheatrical.com.au

New Zealand: Play Bureau, PO Box 9013, St Clair, Dunedin 9047, *tel* (3) 455 9959, *email* info@playbureau.com

USA and Canada: Hatch Talent Ltd, see details below

Professional Performing Rights   Applications for performance by professionals in any medium and in any language throughout the world (including by stock companies in the USA and Canada) should be addressed to Hatch Talent Ltd, 113 Shoreditch High Street, London E1 6JN

No performance of any kind may be given unless a licence has been obtained. Applications should be made before rehearsals begin. Publication of this play does not necessarily indicate its availability for amateur performance.

Woodland CARBON
www.woodlandcarbon.co.uk
NICK HERN BOOKS
Printed on Carbon Captured paper

www.nickhernbooks.co.uk

facebook.com/nickhernbooks

twitter.com/nickhernbooks